Feed The Good Wolf

MATT S. LAW

One of the joys of self-publishing is that I can use this little section of text for whatever purpose I choose. So instead of some boring logistical data or publishing information I plant Easter eggs for people to find. If, for example, you are one of the people who received an autographed copy of this book for free, by finding my secret message in this same spot in my first book, then congratulations on your observational skills and willingness to send me an email for free stuff. But of course I can't hide a free giveaway in the exact same spot now can I? To get a free copy of my next book, you will need to decipher a set of clues hidden in each chapter of this book. Each clue will lead to a spot in the United States where a piece of a key will be hidden in a labyrinth behind a series of death traps, each more dangerous than the last. The fully assembled key then must be brought to the Lincoln Memorial where... I've probably lost you, haven't I? Subscribe to my blog, I'll give away ten copies of my next book to ten of my followers.

DEDICATION

This book is dedicated to my best friend Jason Chapman, who helped feed my good wolf during our childhood together.

Also to the leaders of Worldwide Group, LLC, the greatest organization in the world for developing people into men and women of excellence and character. Continue always "to impact our generation and generations to come with the truth that God created us for greatness" (from the Worldwide Group mission statement).

CONTENTS

1 **Tale of Two Wolves**   1

a Native American parable on character.

2 **Reading**   9

add value to your life

3 **Listening**   19

listen to inspiration and information

4 **Speaking**   30

do not just speak your mind, mind your speech

5 **Association**   39

surround yourself with quality people

6 **Environment**   50

make your surroundings inspire you

7 **Rest**   61

reflect, refocus, replenish, and reward yourself

8 **Principles**   69

live by principle not by popularity

9 **Starve the Bad Wolf**   81

the second half of the equation

10 **Final Thoughts**   88

TALE OF TWO WOLVES

Wise men say that within our hearts are two wolves. One is the bad wolf. It is full of greed, laziness, fear, hatred, jealousy, rage, sorrow. All the negative emotions. The other is the good wolf. It is full of joy, love, kindness, forgiveness, peace of mind. All the positive emotions. Both wolves war against each other continuously in our hearts.

When asked which wolf is stronger, the wise men answer, "Whichever wolf you have been feeding."

This is an adaptation of a Cherokee legend and like most stories that survive through the ages, it is full of ancient wisdom.

Every day we make decisions. Most of these are small, inconsequential decisions, like what to eat for lunch. But on occasion, we are required to make a moral decision; a decision with real consequences; a choice between right and wrong. Selfishness or selflessness. Cruelty or kindness. Jealousy or generosity. Deceit or honesty. And while we may think of ourselves as people of good character most of the time, that can change when we are put to the test. What is really within us is revealed under stress or duress. And whether or not we make the right decision in that split second, is based on which wolf is currently winning the fight in our heart.

And that is dependent on which wolf you have been feeding.

When I talk about the war in your heart, what I'm really talking about is your character. The sum total of the features and qualities that define you as an individual. Character is who you are behind closed doors. Most people spend all their time concerned about their reputation, all the while neglecting or remaining unconcerned with their character.

Your inner heart, your true character, determines what comes out of you during a crisis. The behavior you display during moments of panic, at times of haste, or while under pressure or duress reveals your character; when you don't have time to pass your response through the appropriate social filters. If your first reaction to a crisis is to curse, blame, and point fingers, then that is a sign of what's inside your heart; a sign of weak character. If your first reaction is to assess, analyze, then attack the problem, then you are probably a person of strong moral character.

In other words, I'm not impressed with someone that is calm and rational during a routine lunch. I am impressed with someone that is calm and rational after pulling themselves out of a flaming car wreck, or mass layoffs at their corporation, or a loved one going through an emotional trauma, or all of the above.

Some people might be under the misguided impression that they can compartmentalize their character. They think they can be one person at work, then be another for their wife, and another person entirely at church. Of course they rationalize that it's OK to swear and curse at home and at the office, as long as they don't do it in church. Perhaps some men believe that it is fine to lie and cheat and steal at the office, as long as they are honest where it's important: at home with the wife and kids. Compare them to that other group of men that believe it's alright to lie on occasion to their wives, as long as they are honest with their clients and customers. Which group is right?

Leadership expert John Maxwell once said "There is no such thing as business ethics. There is just ethics." Everything you say to your wife, everything you say at church and everything that you say in your business all have one thing in common: You.

You cannot rationalize that you are a person of right character while performing wrong actions. You are still feeding your bad wolf along with the good.

Location and context does not diminish the fact that you are doing wrong. Ultimately you are tarnishing your character, and along with it your credibility, your integrity, your sense of self-worth. Despite changing your social masks, you are still the same person in each of those situations. Just because the behavior is out of sight of certain people, you still carry your character with you. If you think that it doesn't matter, then consider this:

Would you want your daughter to go out with a young man that was a perfect gentleman when he shook your hand and introduced himself, but the instant he took off with her he transformed into a misogynistic drunkard? Is it fair to judge him on his behavior when he's not in your home? Darn right it is, because he's dating your daughter!

What happened? Why is it acceptable for you to wear two masks but not for the young man courting your daughter? Because there is no such thing as just business ethics, or just family ethics, or just church ethics. There is ethics. We are not interested in a good mask, or a good costume, or a good script. We want to associate with people of good character. We especially want our daughters to meet a man of good character.

Recognize that our behavior away from observers is still part of us. That it is something that will eventually bleed through from one aspect of our life to the others that we're trying to conceal it from.

A man is literally what he thinks, his character being the complete sum of all his thought.
~James Allen

Character is not a sometimes thing. It is not a front for the boss, the wife, or the pastor. Character is an always thing. "The sum total of the features and qualities that define you as an individual." But these things are not predetermined by fate. You are not a slave to your character. You determine your character.

You do that by feeding the good wolf or feeding the bad wolf.

But how do we do that?

Perhaps you've seen this demonstration before. I was sitting in some science class or another and watching a video (a black and white video, so it was a pretty old film) of a visual demonstration of the chain reaction caused by splitting an atom. In the video, was a room full of mousetraps that each had a ping pong ball on it. If one of the mouse traps is triggered, it snaps violently, shooting the ping pong ball away in one direction and flinging itself in another direction. An instant later, the entire room is full of snapping, hopping mousetraps and high-velocity ping pong balls shooting in all directions.

It was an impressive display, and I can only imagine how long it took to set a thousand mousetraps baited with ping pong balls, but what's the point of bringing this up now? Most people picture their own minds like that room full of ping pong balls. They feel that they can't control their thoughts; that their thoughts are just randomly bouncing around in their heads with all the focus and attention span of a ferret. They feel that they have no real power to control what occupies their minds.

That is a lie. We can control our thoughts. We control what we think about by controlling the input.

You determine your character by controlling your thoughts. You control your thoughts by controlling the input to your brain. You control what goes into your own head by determining for yourself what you read, what you watch, who you listen to, who you associate with. And when you are confronted by something which does not mesh with the values that you want to live your life by, you choose to walk away.

That is what is meant by feeding the good wolf.

Our minds are like a computer. A computer is modeled after the human brain. If we want our computer to generate art, we load an art program into it. If we want it to sing and make music we load a karaoke program. We can apply the same simple principle to programming the computer inside our head. If we want our brain to generate prosperity, then we watch television and drink beer, right? Wrong. We read financial magazines and books, seek advice from financially prosperous people, and develop plans and habits to improve our own financial situation. If you want to have a good attitude, you need to think positive thoughts. To think positive thoughts, you need to load positive into your brain. If you want to be successful you need to think about success; to think about success you need to feed your computer success programs and information.

You need to take responsibility for what goes into your own brain.

Most of the world is negative. Television, news, celebrity magazines: Negative. School, work, driving on the freeway during rush hour: Negative. You are completely surrounded by hostile thoughts that are trying to corrupt your hard drive. That's why there is a market for positive mental attitude books and motivational seminars. We're trying to undo all the damage that society has inflicted on you over the course of your life.

If you always have a negative outlook, are constantly condescending, always expect the worst possible scenario, then you have been letting society feed your wolves.

Why all this talk about character? Isn't that old fashioned and dated? Society today is all about results, achievement, getting ahead in a dog-eat-dog world.

Have you already forgotten about that boy dating your daughter?

You want your potential son-in-law to be someone of good character, so they don't cheat on, abuse, or neglect your daughter. You want your employer or employee to be a person of character, so they don't rip you off. You want character in your dentist, your doctor, your candlestick maker.

How much better would this country be if every man and woman for the next ten years made a conscious decision to develop, build, refine and polish their character? If every single person took a solemn vow to become more honest, more responsible, more disciplined, more accepting of others? Obviously, if everyone made that decision, life and society would improve in just about every conceivable way.

I will hazard a guess and say that it is highly unlikely that every person on Earth will make that decision this weekend. Also, you cannot force that decision on every person on Earth. You couldn't even force it on all your neighbors. You probably couldn't even force it on your immediate family members. You can teach them, you can encourage them, but ultimately only they can choose for themselves which wolf to feed.

So you cannot control other people; and you cannot force them to have character. So why not begin with the only person you can control: You.

Once you recognize that you desire people of good character around you, you should recognize the value of working on your own character.

7

By being a person of character you become a more desirable spouse, parent, dentist, doctor, or candlestick maker. As a man or woman of character you become a person of influence. Someone that can raise the bar for your peers. More than anything else, you have friends and family members that need a good example in their life, rather than another beer-drinking buddy.

Of all the properties which belong to honorable men, not one is so highly prized as that of character.
~Henry Clay

So that is the purpose of this book. To teach people to develop good character by being selective about feeding the good wolf in your heart. Each chapter covers a particular form of input into the brain and offers explanations and suggestions for sowing into your thought life.

To change the world, first change your character
To change your character, first change your thoughts
To change your thoughts, feed the good wolf in your heart.

READING

Reading is one of the greatest and most effective methods of adding value to your life and feeding the good wolf. As an author, it might be self-serving of me to make that claim, but it's true.

In any discussion of adding positive input into your mental computer, reading needs to be at the top of the list. Reading is effective for many reasons. One reason is because of its availability. Books are easy to get, inexpensive, and you can read just about anywhere provided you are not driving or operating heavy machinery. With advancements in print-on-demand technology, the number of books being published each year is increasing dramatically. With the widespread use of computers, tablets, and e-readers the availability of eBooks continues to increase exponentially.

Reading is a tremendous tool for learning because it arrests your attention and forces you to live in the moment. It utilizes your brain enough to force you to focus on the words on the page, while at the same time it compels you to create the scene or situation in your own mind that the author describes. It forces you to think and to focus on the subject matter of the words.

Remember the ping pong balls? Remember the chaotic snapping and flinging? Wasn't that awesome? Some of you are just now realizing that you never actually saw that video. You just pictured it in your own mind. In fact, some of you may have remembered that I said that the video I watched was in black and white, so you actually imagined the scene in black and white. And if you didn't before, you most likely did just now when I reminded you. Even if you didn't see the same video I did, you can picture it in your mind, in living black and white.

Rewind that ping-pong ball scene in your head and start it from the beginning. Everything is perfectly still, just thousands of ping pong balls perched on their mousetrap. Toss a single ping-pong ball into the room to set off the chain reaction. Within seconds, everything is chaos and confusion, black and white, snaps and bounces.

Freeze the room. Everything stops in mid-flight. Carefully reach out to one of the ping-pong balls in front of you at shoulder height. Take the permanent marker out of your pocket, and draw a large blue "X" on that ball. Carefully set your ball back into the spot where it was frozen. Now, unfreeze the room, and everything returns to random chaos except for your ball with the "X" which does not move. Everything is a black and white blur of motion except for your ball that is fixed in place and doesn't move.

Continue to focus on that blue "X" for ten more seconds while everything begins slowing down, losing momentum. For another twenty seconds as everything around it just eventually returns to stillness.

The whole point of that surreal scene was to illustrate how reading focuses your thoughts. When our mind is bombarded with sensory input from the outside world (noise, signs, advertisements, traffic jams and annoying commercial jingles), our heads are like that room full of ping-pong balls; stray thoughts bouncing crazily.

But reading requires enough mental focus to recognize words and to string them into sentences sufficiently to comprehend them. That's why I say that reading "arrests your attention." Your thoughts become like that single blue "X," and you remain focused on that while you read, sometimes to the exclusion of the real world. Have you ever been lost in a great novel before? Do you have a friend or family member that can never hear you talking unless you take away whatever they are reading? I rest my case.

When you read, you suspend your own thoughts and allow the author to direct your thinking. Like just now when I made you think about a black and white scene of ping pong balls and mouse traps.

Since you're entrusting me with your brain for this brief moment I want to do everything I can to direct you in a positive way. It's also why I don't write horror fiction anymore.

How to get the most out of reading. I was trained all through grade school to treat my books like library books. After all, they had to be returned to the school at the end of the year, preferably in the same condition they were issued to me in. I carried that habit into college, where I would try to keep my books in excellent condition so that they could be sold back to the bookstore at the end of the year. That's a fine strategy if your goal is to preserve your book. But let me offer this as an alternative goal with your book: learn from it!

When you buy a book it is yours. Mark it up. Underline portions that are important to you. Highlight words, phrases, passages, paragraphs. Write notes in the margins. Write your name on the inside cover. It is your property, beat it up as much as you like. The point is not of course to abuse the book for the sake of proving your superiority over it, but you want to get as much out of it as you can. Also, do not abuse your eReader in this way.

One only reads well when one reads with some quite personal goal in mind.
~Paul Valery

Develop a strategy for reading non-fiction books. I should point out that I differentiate between reading for leisure and reading for study or for personal development. You probably don't need to use these techniques for reading fantasy novels. But when reading self growth books, I personally want to get the most out of it when I read it. I read with purpose. I am searching for lessons and wisdom that I can incorporate into my life, or that I can quote for a future book. I have a hard time reading if I don't have a pen or a highlighter in my hand so that I can mark sentences that I feel are profound. Having that pen in hand also helps me to focus; it's a reminder that I am actively searching not passively scanning. It's like hunting for knowledge with a tiny, florescent, plastic spear. If I think a particular sentence is really profound, I will type it into my smartphone and email it to myself to keep it on file. This is much easier than trying to remember the book and author that the quote was from later.

Different readers have different reading strategies. During a Leadership conference, John C. Maxwell described his system for reading. He highlights important passages, but for extremely important messages he will transcribe them onto an index card and put them into a quote file. He also writes notes in the margin next to important ideas using his personal notation system: "A" for ideas that he needs to Apply to his life/teaching, "C" for ideas that he needs to Change, "T" for ideas he needs to Teach his leaders/employees.

The head pastor of one of the mega-churches in my hometown shared the reading strategy that he uses. When he first acquires a new book, the first thing he does is create a three-column index on the inside cover or on a blank page. This way, when he highlights important ideas, he can record the page number, the subject, and a brief excerpt in the index. Also, he highlights the very edge of the pages that have important quotes on them, this way it's much easier to flip through the book later and find those quotes. This is a simple, fantastic idea that I wish I had started implementing about two hundred books ago.

Michael Hyatt, expert on social media platform-building and intentional leadership, recorded a podcast summarizing his ten Best Practices for Reading Non-Fiction Books. Many of them I've already mentioned, but two that stood out to me are:

1. Don't feel you need to finish.
9. Review the book and transfer actions to a to-do list.

The first point is important because by its very nature, a book is written to as large an audience as possible. Not everything in it will be applicable to you as an individual. Look for those ideas that you can best apply to your own life. And the ninth point is important because too often when we finish a book we immediately continue on to our next project and don't take the time to meditate and contemplate the message we read. Too often, we finish a book, think it's great, then forget about it a week later. Once the book is out of sight it's out of mind. By transferring the most important bullet points to something that we keep, such as our planner or daily schedule, we can effect change from the knowledge we gather.

Reread Books. I reread a lot of books in my personal library, and it is astonishing to me after the passage of a few years how I missed so many gems of wisdom the first time through. Also, how some of the things that I thought were important then, really aren't that great now. Rereading an old book that you have highlighted and marked up is a great way to gauge your growth since you last read it. Also, just recently I came up with the brilliant idea to use a different color highlighter each time I read a book, so that I can compare what I thought was important then to what I think is important now.

Here's a sentence from *As A Man Thinketh* by James Allen. I am including it here for no other reason than I grabbed the closest book to me and flipped through it until I found a section that was double-highlighted. Here's what I came up with, highlighted in yellow and also underlined in red:

> *Let a man radically alter his thoughts, and he will be astonished at the rapid transformation it will effect in the material conditions of his life.*

See how profound that was? Thankfully, it is also pertinent to the subject of my book.

Benefits of Reading. Reading helps you to focus mentally. I went through most of my high school years being a very ineffective reader. I could read, just with very little comprehension and retention. Perhaps you can relate to this scenario: Read a few sentences, stop because you realize that you have no idea what you were just reading, start over reading from the beginning of the last paragraph. Actually, in high school I skipped that last part, and never bothered going back over something I didn't understand (and my GPA reflected that).

My problem was mainly that I was reading for the sake of reading. I was required to read chapter X because a teacher told me to. When I finally began reading with the goal of learning, I would actually go back and see what I missed when my attention fuzzed out. Over time, I got better. I'm not a speed reader today; and I don't have a photographic memory. But after reading a little bit, nearly every day for fifteen plus years, I was bound to improve.

Reading helps to cultivate your creativity and imagination. When you read, your mind turns words into images. The author tells the story, but you are the director of your own little movie studio in your brain. My visual ping pong ball metaphor with the blue X is a perfect example. When you imagined that scene, I am willing to bet that your inner mind visualized details that I never included. I never specified the size of the "X" you figured that out on your own. But that's alright. As the director, you're allowed to take creative liberties with my work in order to make it your own.

Imagination is a powerful tool for shaping your character. Creating and holding a vivid picture in your mind will invariably cause you to move in the direction of your thought. There are entire books devoted to this idea, some of them religious and spiritual, some of them secular and psychological. Read *Creative Visualization* by Shakti Gawain. Read *Think and Grow Rich* by Napolean Hill. Read *As A Man Thinketh* by James Allen. Read *The Science of Getting Rich* by Wallace Wattles. Read *Psycho-Cybernetics* by Maxwell Maltz. Also read *How To Win Friends and Influence People* by Dale Carnegie. Actually that last one is totally unrelated to the subject, but I swore in my first book that I would recommend this book to people every chance I get. The point is, that your thoughts guide the direction of your life, and the exercise of reading strengthens your ability to formulate strong, clear, convincing thoughts.

Be selective with your reading. Words have power, and anything you read is like a direct line into your brain from the author. That's why I read books that I think will empower me, uplift me, give me knowledge that I need to improve on or grow in some way. I'm not saying that you should never read for leisure any more. Just value your time. Time spent reading a positive, motivating, inspirational book is time that is invested in your character and your future. Time spent reading fiction is hobby time (unless you are a fiction writer in which case I would call that time "research").

Here is a brief glimpse into my own personal reading plan:
I have a queue of books that I am currently reading that I selected because of certain goals that I set for this month. I am in the process of developing myself as a leader and influencer of people. For that reason I picked out

two books by John C. Maxwell to read: *Developing the Leader Within You* and *Developing the Leaders Around You*. The first to work on myself, and the second because eventually, to complete the vision that I currently have for my life, will require more than just me. I will need a team of people, and I will need to help them develop into leaders as well. I later added an additional book by John, *The 21 Irrefutable Laws of Leadership*. Even though this is a book on the same subject matter and covers similar material, this book is more recent, and even John Maxwell is continually learning and improving himself. So I want to hear his newest insights and experiences. I also have *Dare to Discipline Yourself*, by Dale E. Galloway in the queue, because I know myself and I have a tendency to drift towards laziness. I want to be more disciplined in my daily activities and habits, from my writing work habit to my physical fitness to my organization of my office and home. And after that, is *Influence: Science and Practice* by Robert B. Cialdini, Ph.D. This book was recommended to me by an acquaintance about a year back, and when he suggested it, I realized that I had already read it in college. It was on the required reading list for a speech class I was taking, and for some reason, I remember it being good enough that I elected to hold onto it and keep it rather than try to sell it back to the bookstore at the end of the semester. At the conclusion of five years of college, I only held on to three of my books—and the other two were simply because the bookstore didn't want them anymore. I had forgotten all about this book, but now I want to read it again; both because someone recommended it to me and because College Matt thought it was good enough to keep.

I usually read three to four books on personal development each month. At the beginning of each month, I am trying to be more purposeful in selecting books to develop myself in a particular area. This month is leadership and influence. But in the past I have read books on communication skills, books on success principles, books on the power of the tongue, books on marital relationships. I am passionate about continually growing myself.

Reading is one of the greatest things you can do for yourself to become a better you. Develop a regular reading habit. In fact, develop a love affair with reading. Just make sure you are reading material that is feeding the good wolf not the bad wolf.

LISTENING

Listening to a person is important. But listening to the right people is more important. We gather knowledge from listening to sermons, to class lectures, to stories. We receive encouragement from friends, from family members, from loved ones. Unfortunately you can't always have positive friends, mentors and business colleagues following you around to speak wisdom and encouragement into you. But you can still listen to words of wisdom from the foremost experts on such important subjects as leadership, positive mental attitude, time management, finances, salesmanship, introductory French, and conversational Klingon. All of these subjects have experts, and these experts make audio recordings of their teachings, and make them available to the public by selling them.

Some of you may be horrified that experts would sell their advice to the public. Remember, you don't have to take advice from experts. Advice is both abundant and free of charge, from those people who are not qualified to charge for it. Broke people are very quick to offer financial advice. Don't take it. Adulterers are also quick to offer marital advice. Drunkards are quick to offer advice on leisure activity. Actually drunkards are quick to offer advice on just about any topic; quickly, loudly, and uninvited.

So yes, there are experts that allow you to learn from them, if for no other reason than to protect you from the teachings of the rest of the world. The majority of the world is negative. In order to feed your good wolf, you need to acquire the habit of listening to positive people.

When I first got involved in business development, soon after graduating from college, my business partners encouraged me to listen to as many audio cassettes as possible from successful business owners. (For my younger readers, these "audio cassettes" were the precursor to "compact discs"). (For my even younger readers, "compact discs" were the precursor to "MP3s"). Some of the tapes were for teaching purposes; let's classify them as "instructional" and/or "informational." Many of the other tapes were for the purpose of developing a proper positive attitude or mindset; let's call them "motivational" and/or "inspirational."

I wanted to learn how to get ahead, and I thought I needed more instruction and information for that. So I listened primarily to the instructional tapes. I wanted to know about processes, techniques, logistics; all the "how to" of creating a business, building a client base, planning, processes, pitches.

I didn't start to see any significant results in business though until I started listening to the motivational and inspirational speakers. In fact, it was recommended to me that I listen to five inspirational tapes for every informational tape I listened to.

Why was that? Because attitude is more important than knowledge in most business endeavors. If you've ever worked in sales, you've probably heard the phrase "ignorance on fire is better than knowledge on ice." A fired up, enthusiastic salesman will sell more than a well-informed, robotic one. Enthusiasm is contagious. Lists of data, rarely so. And I needed to work on being less robotic.

Also, learning all the "how to" of a business does not necessarily position you for success. People that understand "How" will usually end up as an employee working for a person that understands "Why." A powerful reason, a strong "Why" trumps a lack of "How." Motivation will beat information almost every time.

Most of the positive attitude tapes I listened to were people recounting "their story" of how they succeeded: building their business, facing adversity, improving their relationships and their lives. Most people called it their testimony. If this were a business class it would be called a case study.

At first I didn't see the value of listening to other people talk about where they came from, how they succeeded, and how great their life is now. The value is this:

Listening to success stories allows you to share in the victory (assuming of course that you are not a petty, jealous person). Hearing someone describe the benefits and rewards of their success allows you to visualize yourself in the same or a similar position. Picturing victory is an important part of achieving victory.

Listening to success stories expands your thinking. Listen to a successful person talk about their life and learn also about the serendipities that come with success. You might be surprised how achieving financially eliminates a significant number of other family or marital challenges. Or you may be surprised at how often restoring a relationship with your spouse improves your situation in business. Or how developing a proper vertical alignment, placing God first in your life, will positively impact every other area of your life. You may learn that success adds more than just stability to your life, but also significance. Learning from successful people opens your mind to possibilities that you may have not even considered. New possibilities, lead to an increase in desire, which in turn increases your passion, which drives you toward success.

Listening to success stories helps you overcome challenges. I promise you, that in any endeavor of significance that you attempt in your life, you will at some point have a person, event or situation stand in the way of your achievement. All success requires overcoming adversity. Hearing someone tell you how they faced their challenges can teach you not only to expect obstacles but to expect the overcoming of obstacles as a normal part of the success journey.

Sometimes you may gain specific insight on how to overcome an obstacle of your own. But even if the person you are listening to is speaking on a totally different subject or industry than yours, stories of overcoming instill within us the attitude that we can also face and slay our own dragons.

A friend of mine that manages a team of professional salesmen plays the theme song from Rocky for his sales force before unleashing them onto the floor. Why? Because the Rocky movies and even the theme song itself has become synonymous with overcoming, victory, triumph. And none of his salesmen have ever had to fight a prospect!

Also, hearing about a challenge that someone else conquered will often break us out of the habit of making excuses for failure. I would have a hard time believing that I'm out of shape because of a sprained ankle twelve years ago after listening to the story of a blind man who ran a marathon with no legs. I can't believe that the reason I'm not more successful financially is because I have no start-up capital after listening to a multimillionaire who arrived in the country five years ago with $60 in his pocket and not able to read or speak English.

Personal success stories allow us to visualize another human being overcoming difficulty, hardship, and sometimes tragedy. That is the basis of a winning attitude: the ability to overcome obstacles and challenges.

Begin building a personal library of audio recordings. There are many different professional speakers, covering a wide range of topics and each with their own personal style. Listen to a variety of speakers on a variety of subjects. The more you have, the more you can mix up your playlist. If you only own a single CD ("compact disc" for my younger readers), no matter how good the speaker is, you'll grow weary of listening to it eventually. Just like you would probably stop going to the movies if every theater only played *The Sound of Music* all day every day.

Some speakers you will relate to. Some you will trust. Some you will not for some absurd reason like they have a slight Jamaican accent and it bugs you. That's why you should listen to different speakers. Because eventually one speaker will say something in a voice that will make you believe that one key point that you've been waiting for. It may be something you've heard many times before, but believe for the first time when this particular speaker tells it to you.

Listening to a broad range of speakers also helps you to connect with people. A vital skill in communication and in relationships is the ability to connect with people. Hearing stories of success from different speakers' perspectives, gives you the ability to relate to people of different backgrounds. This was especially important for myself as a young man just out of college. It allowed me to hear life experiences from people of different ages, different occupations, of a different gender or race or upbringing.

Whenever you meet with a person, you want to try to establish a connection with them. If you have some kind of common ground, it is easier to develop a rapport; and eventually trust and friendship. It's easy if you both went to the same college, grew up in the same state, belong to the same church, or vacationed in the same country. But for a young kid fresh out of college with no real life experience, I didn't have a lot of commonality with anyone outside my neighborhood.

Listening to speakers with diverse backgrounds allows you to draw knowledge from their backgrounds. You may not become an expert just from listening to a few recorded speeches, but you should be able to pick up enough information to be able to ask questions that aren't stupid.

In addition to speeches, lectures and seminars, books are available in audio format as well. Personally, I don't normally listen to audio books for several reasons. First, because I prefer to read. Second, like most people, I read faster than most people speak, so reading takes me less time. Third, you typically retain less info listening than by reading and I'd rather get as much out of it as I can the first time through. Fourth, I've been told that sometimes the written word loses something in the transition to the spoken word. Possibly it loses that magic ring of truth you feel when you are creating the words yourself in your own internal voice. While that may be a lot of negative points about audio books, the bottom line is: I would rather listen to an audio book than to heavy metal music. Audio books are an available option for those that are constantly on the go and don't have the time to sit and read; or for those that have difficulty reading (I am constantly meeting very successful people that struggled with dyslexia growing up, so that is another excuse that doesn't hold water).

Develop a listening strategy. I very rarely listen to music anymore, but recently on a road trip in a rental car, I tuned the radio to an 80's music station. There are many songs from that era that I still knew all the words to, even though I haven't heard them in over twenty years. Truth be told, that irritated me a little. I would like to think that my brain is being used for something more productive than memorizing lyrics to songs that don't make any sense. So how did I permanently burn these words into my memory? A combination of focus and repetition.

Most people are terrible listeners. According to professional motivator Zig Ziglar, you retain only about 10% of what you hear in a speech. When a man who made a living as a professional speaker tells you that you are only going to retain about 10% of what he's saying, you can probably believe him. Listening is usually passive, and since we are not actively engaging in conversation when we are listening to a recording or a lecture, it is easy for our mind to wander. You will get more out of an audio presentation if you have some kind of activity that keeps your mind focused on the speaker.

The reason I remember all those song lyrics, is because like most nerds in grade school, I would write out song lyrics in my Biology notebook. Some of them I memorized by reading the lyrics on the album cover; but the ones I really remember word for word twenty years later are the ones that I had to translate myself by carefully listening and transcribing each line. That took a lot of focus (although not as much as translating 90's music I'd wager).

In college, I got excellent grades in my lecture classes because I was a good note-taker. Since I knew I wasn't going to read the text book, it was vital that I got all the information from the professor during those three hours a week. So I scribbled notes furiously. Anything that you write down gets anchored into your memory much better than anything you read or anything you hear.

So to really focus on listening, and get the most out of an audio recording, you should sit in a quiet place and take notes.

The other half of that equation is repetition. I received Zig Ziglar's lecture series entitled *See You at the Top* years ago from my father (so long ago it was on audio cassette tapes). In it, Mr. Ziglar encourages his audience to listen to the entire series seven to ten times in order to really learn it. Seven to ten times? And this was a twelve tape set. That is a large investment of time. But remember, if you only retain 10% of what you hear, even listening to something 7 times only brings you up to about a 70% retention rate (that's not actually true). The point is though, that repetition helps to imprint the learning into your brain.

Repetition was the key to me remembering all those song lyrics. Whenever a hit song made it onto the radio in my day, it got repeated over and over until the public was sick of it. That's how we remember those old song lyrics and also why most of us can repeat commercial jingles and company slogans that haven't been on the air for twenty years. Cumulative input compounds memorization.

Develop a listening schedule. I generally assume, that if you live in the U.S., then you are busy. Incorporate your listening time into your daily life not during "free time," which is a rare commodity for us, but during your "brainless time." Most of your daily routine can be accomplished without the use of your brain. You are on auto-pilot through most of your morning routine. Put a tape player, CD player, or digital audio device of some sort into your bathroom. While you are in the shower, brushing your teeth, shaving, or taking care of other bathroom business: listen! Your brain is not doing anything productive, so you might as well have some positive, motivational speakers putting life into you. Just don't get your electronic devices wet. Listen to motivational speakers while you are washing the dishes, vacuuming the carpets, or folding your laundry. Get some headphones and listen to positive while you are shopping, running errands, or exercising. There is no reason for you to leave your brain in idle for so many hours each day.

For informational or instructional audio recordings you may need to schedule out some actual "free time" or "non-productive time" to listen to those. If the audio you are listening to is loaded up with a lot of facts and knowledge that you are trying to memorize, then allowing it to play in the background might not be the best way to retain that information. For those, you will probably want to sit, listen, and take notes.

Here's my personal method for successful listening:
I have a substantial library of digital files and audio CDs of many different business leaders and motivational speakers. Since moving into the digital age, I've shifted to storing recordings on my smartphone, which has become my all-in-one: phone, calendar, notepad, and digital recorder/playing device.

I will usually transfer six to eight recordings at a time onto my phone, listen through all of them 2 or 3 times, then swap them out for some fresh material about two weeks later.

I personally opt for "repetition" rather than "focus" as my main learning mechanism when it comes to listening to audio. This is because, if I have enough free time to sit down with a pen and take notes, I would prefer to use that time for either reading or writing.

My phone is my alarm clock. Once I turn off my alarm in the morning, I switch it to play mode and carry it around with me as I proceed to wake up. I listen while I shower in the morning. Most of us don't expend much mental concentration to shower, it just kind of happens. The only challenge I had when I first tried this is the speaker on my phone isn't very loud, so I had a hard time hearing it from the bathroom counter. Solution: I seal the phone in a plastic bag and place it in the shower with me. Sure, they make water-proof shower stereos, but I prefer old-school, common-sense solutions (also, cheap).

The advantage of keeping my daily play-list of positive on my phone is that I carry it with me at all times. It stays on while I get dressed in the morning and begin my day. When I drive, I plug my phone into my dashboard, hit play, and suddenly my car is a mobile university of success. I also keep a pair of earphones in my car so that I can continue to listen when my day advances beyond the confines of my car.

You don't always need to whittle time out of your existing schedule. Sometimes you can simply re-designate those auto-pilot hours into self-improvement hours; let those hours automatically feed your good wolf.

SPEAKING

Speaking your mind is not nearly as important as minding your speech.
~Matt S. Law (unless someone, somewhere can prove that they wrote it first).

Listening and reading are two important and easily accessible ways to feed the good wolf. Listening is primarily passive. Reading is a more active method that more fully engages the imagination. Speech is an active and deliberate method of feeding the good wolf; and is probably the most powerful.

Anything you say has a direct connection with your conscious mind. Anything you repeatedly speak sinks into the subconscious mind. The act of speaking fully arrests your attention just as reading does, except you are the ultimate author of the words you speak. That way you are not needlessly subjected to ping-pong ball visual metaphors from someone trying to make a point. Just decide for yourself what the point is that you want to instill into your thoughts, or character, then state your point.

Follow my reasoning here:

Your character is the sum total of your thoughts.

Anything you articulate into words, your mind must think on.

Therefore, your speech is directly inputting into your character.

That was important so let me repeat that.: *Your speech is direct input into your character.*

In fact, you should stop what you are doing and post that to all of your social media accounts right now (be sure to attribute to @Matt_S_Law).

I have heard many authors and speakers say "what you speak is what you get." I would take this one step further and say "what you speak is what you become." That is why I have a low tolerance for self-deprecating humor from people that I care about.

Guard your negative speech. If I hear a friend or co-worker insult themselves, I tell them matter-of-factly: "Stop. If somebody else were to make those same comments about you, I would beat the crap out of them."

The typical response is "Well, it's alright because it's just me saying it."

No it is not. It's a hundred times worse.

A wonderful woman that I used to work with had a terrible habit of insulting herself, and it reached the point where our co-workers would pile on and add to the insults; including the manager of the store (one of my early experiences confirming that leadership has little to do with a title). I finally had a talk with her at the end of her shift. I told her (although probably not as cogently as I'm recounting it here): "Lisa, (not her real name) you are one of the sweetest people I have ever met. I have never heard you say an unkind or malicious word about anyone. Except when you talk about yourself." I gave her a copy of *The Tongue: A Creative Force* by Charles Capps, and tried to explain that every negative statement about herself is insulting a creation of God and also placing her under a curse. I haven't seen her for many years now, but I hope that day had an impact on her. She did give me a Thank You card that I still have to this day.

What goes into someone's mouth does not defile them, but what comes out of their mouth, that is what defiles them.
~Matthew 15:11

While speech directly inputs into our thoughts, and subsequently our character, the opposite is also true. Our speech reveals our character. When we do not make the effort to police what comes out of our mouth, what is in our hearts and minds comes spilling out.

For the mouth speaks what the heart is full of.
~Matthew 12:34

If you say something while intoxicated that you wouldn't normally say to someone's face, your character is exposed. You are revealed as a liar, trust is destroyed, the relationship is tarnished. Even if you apologize later, no one really believes that it was "the liquor talking." There is a seed of truth in the Latin phrase "In Vino Veritas"; "in wine (there is the) truth."

Of course it doesn't require impaired judgment from alcohol to cause destruction with your mouth. You can inflict the same damage by blurting out an insult that is meant as a joke. However you want to spin it, teasing someone is simply an attempt to boost your own social standing at the expense of the other person's self-esteem. The more you have to say "just kidding" or accompany your text messages with "j/k" the weaker your integrity. A chronic insulter is someone of both low self-esteem and shoddy character.

> *Like a maniac shooting flaming arrows of death, is one who deceives their neighbor and says, "I was only joking!"*
> ~Proverbs 26:18-19

The person subjected to your comment is usually expected to be a good sport, to not take it personally, to shrug off demeaning remarks. If societal norms expect your target to be a good sport and accept your abuse, then how will you know when one of your comments causes genuine pain? Stop limiting your social skills to the teaching of schoolyard bullies and ignoring both the Bible and modern psychiatry.

Anything we speak or hear, we will always carry with us. In the absence of a traumatic brain injury, we never truly forget anything. Every word we speak is stored in the subconscious mind permanently. And our subconscious mind cannot tell the difference between a statement of truth or fiction.

> *Every joke, every cutting remark, every insult becomes a part of us always.*

You had best err on the side of caution and shut up. Guard your idle thoughts and words. Every time we manage to stop a useless or negative phrase from belching out of our own mouth, we are taming the tongue. People that pride themselves on saying unpleasant things and attributing it to speaking the truth are really just people with extremely low self-images that seek to tear down others.

Feed the good wolf with positive speech. I believe I've sufficiently expounded on the dangers of negative speech. However, it is not enough just to "not speak negative." You need to "actively speak positive." You need to sow seeds of growth and life into yourself with your words. You need to sow seeds of virtue and confidence into your family. You need to be purposeful and intentional with your speech to push you forward not to drag you down.

Speech is a form of input into your mind that you have absolute control over. You speak it, you hear it, you think it. We can influence our character, our personality, and even the circumstances in our lives through deliberate, intentional self-talk.

If you are timid, then you can affect your own thoughts and character by repeating these words over and over: "I am bold. I am confident."

If you are ashamed of your lack of achievements up to this point in your life, then repeat to yourself: "I am a champion. I am growing. I am worthy."

If you are fatigued, you can renew yourself by saying: "I am energized, I am alert, every cell in my body is electrified."

If you feel unloved or insignificant, remind yourself how valuable you are by stating: "I am a child of God. I am the son of a king, not the son of a pauper."

You can bolster your own self-confidence with words. It can be done as an emergency measure, like taking mega-doses of Vitamin C right before you are about to catch a cold. You can give yourself a pep-talk before going into a meeting, giving a speech, calling a pretty girl. But the real power of words is in their constant and regular use, like taking your daily vitamins along with a proper diet including fruits and vegetables. By speaking positive words daily, you generate positive thoughts, and nurture your character in a great way.

> *Relentless, repetitive self talk is what changes our self-image.*
> ~Denis Waitley

Design your own personal affirmations. Some people may ridicule the idea of using self-talk or positive affirmations. Ask yourself this question before you accept any advice from them: are those people typically negative about everything? If so, take that as confirmation from God that you are on the right track; and they were derailed at the station.

Words are powerful. All of us have seen the damage of an unkind word. All of us have felt the warmth of a kind phrase. A personal affirmation is a phrase designed to guide us, to strengthen us, to move us toward a predetermined destination. They are positive words designed to work against the vast amount of negative and neutral words that are spoken into us by the rest of the world. By composing our own affirmations, we become intentional about using our speech to design our life.

While carefully and deliberately crafting your personal affirmations, here are some rules to follow:

1. Always phrase in the present tense. Rather than saying "I will be a great athlete," say "I am a great athlete." When you speak affirmations in the present tense, you are forming an image in your mind of your desire. This will cause your subconscious mind to influence your thoughts and actions to proceed in that direction. The words "I will be" or "I'm going to" or "Someday" are words that neuter the effectiveness of whatever affirmation follows it. It creates a mind-image of yourself always "on the way to" your destination rather than "arrived at." Your subconscious mind has nowhere to guide you to then, since you are already where you instructed it to be.

2. Always use positive statements. Always say "I am a success," not "I will not fail." Your subconscious mind works in images not in strings of words. The phrase "I will not fail" creates a mind-image of yourself failing. Same as if I tell you that you are NOT imagining yourself picking up a wedge of lemon and biting into it right now. Your face probably visibly reacted just now didn't it? Negative statements will work against you not for you.

3. Use your own words. Craft your affirmations in your own voice, your own tone, your own vocabulary. It may be tempting to copy someone else's mission statement out of a book, but for your words to have any effectiveness, they have to have personal meaning to you. By writing your personal affirmations out in your own hand in your own words, you take ownership of them. When you own something, you have a vested interest in it.

4. Speak them out loud. Reading your affirmations to yourself using your internal voice is good. But there is inherent power in the spoken word. Napolean Hill expounds on this in great detail in *Think and Grow Rich* as does Claude Bristol in *The Magic of Believing*. When you speak your affirmations aloud, backed with emotion, you speak with power. You don't have to say them to another living person, but you should still speak them aloud so that you hear it being spoken in your own voice.

You can change your affirmations. You are not stuck with the first thing you write down. You may decide to add something later. In fact, you should expound on your thoughts, come up with specific examples of things that you want. You may decide to remove a goal that you thought was laudable at first but seems asinine now. The goal is to have a list of personal affirmations that you speak with conviction and emotion. You should change your affirmations when they are no longer stated with a deep emotional resolve and instead become rote repetition.

When should you speak your affirmations? Denis Waitley says to be "repetitive" and "relentless." Napolean Hill says you should speak them out loud twice a day; when you retire at night and when you arise in the morning. Og Mandino in his epic book *The Greatest Salesman in the World* instructs the reader to read his magic scrolls (affirmations) at morning and noon, and to read them aloud at night. Claude Bristol in *The Magic of Believing* writes of the "mirror technique" in which you should speak directly into your reflection, staring into your own eyes. If you pray at each meal, say your affirmations when giving thanks.

The more you engage in effective self-talk, the quicker your words embed the image you want into your subconscious mind. Once your subconscious mind is working for you instead of against you, you will begin moving in the direction of the mind-image; and the world will seem to be moving itself and circumstance to help you achieve it.

Personal testimony on my self-talk:
I've always been good at avoiding negative speech (mostly from being an introvert). It is only fairly recently (within the last several years) that I've been forcing myself to actively speak positive words of affirmation to mold my life into the life I want rather than the life I have.

For example, I began repeatedly referring to myself as "Best-selling author, Matt S. Law" long before I had a best-selling book. I didn't introduce myself to people that way, but it was my personal mantra. When I lie in bed at night I would repeat and meditate on those words. "I am a best-selling author. I am a gifted writer with an important message."

I began speaking of (and envisioning myself as) an "expert on the subjects of motivation and personal development" long before I made any significant income as an author, coach or speaker. I visualized myself in the position I wanted, and developed my personal affirmations to enforce that image rather than to undermine it.

Speak your desires into existence. Not just the things that you want to achieve, but the traits and characteristics that you want to have. Make sure every word you speak is feeding the good wolf.

ASSOCIATION

Associate with men of good quality if you esteem your own reputation; for it is
better to be alone than in bad company.
~Booker T. Washington

You are the same today that you are going to be in five years from now except
for two things: the people with whom you associate and the books you read.
~Charles Jones

As a parent... actually I'm not a parent so let me start again. As a child, my parents did their best to keep me away from certain kids. If you're a parent, I'm sure you've done the same thing. Kids that are disrespectful, kids that swear a lot, kids that are bullies, that have violent tendencies, that mistreat puppies. You don't want your child hanging around with them; you don't want your own children to start adopting the behaviors and values of their undesirable peers. We want to insulate our children for as long as possible from bad influences, until they are old enough and wise enough to be able to discern right behavior from wrong. So our parents encouraged us to make friends with the polite, studious, well-behaved kids; rather than the foul-mouthed, car-jacking, drug-peddling crew. And frankly, they didn't care which ones were the cool kids.

As adults, we think that we are immune to the effects of peer pressure, but that is because we are just better at lying to ourselves. If you were to give me half an hour to interview the five people that you spend the most amount of time with on a weekly basis, I could paint a pretty accurate picture of the kind of person you are—without ever talking about you. Your behavior, your beliefs, the music you like, your physical and leisure activities, the kinds of movies and television shows that you watch, are all things that are probably the same as your immediate peer group.

We will become like the people we associate with the most.

You could argue "of course I spend time with people like me. I choose to spend time with them because we have similar values." That may be the case in some instances, but most of the people that we say are our friends are our friends because we were thrown together and forced to spend time together. Most of our long time friends are from our school years. Or people who live near us. Or people we work with. A lot of our friends became friends because of geography rather than values. Think of certain mannerisms or phrases that you use with one friend and not another, then ask yourself "Did I get that from him or did he get that from me?" Even if you think that you are immune to the effects of social imprinting by your friends, then they could have just as easily got their behaviors, beliefs, likes and dislikes from you.

Since we are social creatures, and since we are susceptible to peer pressure, we should try to use peer pressure to our advantage. As responsible adults, it's up to us to make sure we are associating with the good kids.

Associate with many different types of people. Most of us don't have successful, multimillionaire friends with loving family relationships and strong values for us to spend time with and model ourselves after. We are not looking for perfect role-models to associate with. In fact, the closer you get to someone, the more aware of their faults you become. Someone that you may seek out financial advice from may be on his sixth or seventh marriage and have a cocaine addiction that you don't want to emulate. Or someone with an amazing relationship with their spouse may not have the same spiritual values that you do. And I'll bet your church is full of people with genuinely saint-like spiritual walks but you wouldn't want to share their check books.

There are no perfect people, everyone has faults and flaws. You can accept all people; just don't accept advice from all people. Love them for who they are, love them for being children of God; but only accept their counsel in areas of strength.

> *Every man I meet is my master in some point, and in that I learn of him.*
> ~Ralph Waldo Emerson

Guide your daily conversations in positive directions. As Emerson said, every man is your master at something. When you invest your time with people, as often as possible you want that time to be spent in conversation around that person's area of mastery. At the same time, you want to weed out conversations that stray down negative paths like gossip, idleness, and criticism. You want to spend time with people in their area of strength, for two reasons.

First, you benefit and grow from their counsel in that area. Those fictional sample-peers that I mentioned a few paragraphs ago. Despite being flawed individuals, by associating with all three and positively guiding your conversations with them, you can enjoy the wisdom that they offer in financial, relational and spiritual growth. But by allowing the conversations to drift into inane, negative territory, you can learn how to become a divorced, bankrupt drug addict.

> *Plans fail for lack of counsel, but with many advisers they succeed.*
> ~Proverbs 15:22

Second, most people enjoy talking about their own accomplishments. By talking with people in their area of interest or expertise you gain a reputation as a skilled conversationalist; even if all you do is ask questions and let the other person talk.

When a conversation begins to drift in a negative direction, be proactive about getting it back onto a positive course. Here's a solid gold truth you should underline and highlight: The person asking questions is the one controlling the conversation.

When you are having coffee with the top salesman at your company and he points out the girl behind the counter with the truly great anatomy; ask him a question about something else. Ask him how he managed to close his last customer. Ask him how he would handle one of your difficult clients. Ask him where he's planning on spending the bonus that he just got. This changes the subject and pays him a compliment by letting him know that you value his financial advice and achievements.

Be willing to sever ties with people that drag you down. In my first book I wrote about the power of association. Specifically, about how many of us are just one or two relationships away from being able to move ourselves into a successful position in life. Except that sometimes those are one or two relationships that we should end.

Some people are mental and emotional sinkholes. They may well have some qualities that you admire, but they are chronically negative about everything and everyone. If that business friend of yours refuses to talk business unless you take a sniff of cocaine first, walk away. If a man appears to have an incredible relationship with his spouse that you admire, but all he talks about is how stupid you are for believing in God, walk away. If your pastor preaches a sermon every other week criticizing you for being wealthy, bring your tithe to another church.

You can try a few times to turn conversations with those people in a positive direction. But if they continue to dump on your dreams, your values, your personality, then just cut them off. Don't give a speech, just erase their contact information and stop associating with them.

As you begin to personally grow, you will begin to outgrow some people around you. When that happens, there is discomfort in your social group; because someone is trying to be different or do something different. If you don't think that's the case with your friends, try carrying a copy of *How to Win Friends and Influence People* with you to work and see how many react positively and how many ridicule you.

It's not always that the people in your world are totally negative. Most people simply have a knee-jerk reaction to respond contrarily to anything that challenges the status quo. So anytime you change something about yourself, the initial negative comment that some of your friends throw at you are not really negative; they are just clinging to the status quo.

> *Contrarianism is creativity for the untalented.*
> ~Dennis Miller

Depending on your personality, you can either challenge them or ignore them. The people that are truly your friends will accept you. Once you commit to personal growth, you will either pull them up with you, or allow them to drag you down with them. Just remember that you don't make their choices, you can only make choices for yourself.

Your time is valuable, so surround yourself with people that add value to your life, not those that suck life from you. Take an emotional inventory sometime and determine which of your relationships are replenishing and which are depleting. If you want to grow as a person, be discerning about those people that are closest to you and that you spend the most time with.

Actively seek out positive association. A few years back I was surprised to hear that the top three New Year's resolutions that people made were to:

1. lose weight
2. make or save more money
3. make friends with a better class of people

The first two I've heard from plenty of folks. The last is a more recent development in this country I think. People are finally starting to recognize the power of association. Have you noticed an increase in advertising for "mentorship" and "life coaching"? People are looking to upgrade their level of association, but don't know how to go about it. So the profession of life coaching was born.

If you have the money to invest in a life coach, feel free to try it. I personally have no experience to share on the subject. But for those of you on a budget, I would like to point out to you that successful people are much more approachable than the masses seem to think they are. A lot of times we can positively impact our lives just by being friendly and taking an interest in other people.

If you want to start a small business, go to a small business owner in your neighborhood and offer to buy them a cup of coffee so that you can pick their brain for about 15 minutes. If you want to climb the corporate ladder, do the same thing with your manager, or their manager above them, or a manager in a rival company. Remember it is a compliment to them that you value them enough to want to learn from them. Yes, successful people are usually busy, but many truly successful people are willing to take time to encourage success in others.

Just be aware, when you have an opportunity to meet with someone that is successful, do not waste their time. Have a list of questions or subjects that you want to talk about. Value their time; let them know you value their time.

If you want to grow in your spiritual life, go to church (duh). Just remember, there are no perfect churches; and if they ever built one, it would stop being perfect the instant you walked into it. Going to church once a week doesn't fall into the category of "association" so much as "listening." It's more like a college lecture than a counseling session. However, every church I've attended had small groups that met once a week for bible study or fellowship. These are your opportunities to spend time in association with people of like values. If your church doesn't have any, invite some people or families to your home. Offer to take your pastor to lunch on occasion.

If you are looking for a spiritual mentor or role-model in your life, it's important to spend time with them outside of church. Why? Because everyone is pious while they are in church. You need to see if they are walking the spiritual walk while they are in a different environment before you take counsel from them.

If you are looking for new association, consider attending seminars. There are professional speakers and organizations that host lectures, seminars and conventions all over the world. If you are looking to grow financially, relationally or spiritually, I guarantee that somewhere in the country there is an expert on that subject giving a speech or conducting some kind of training seminar that you can attend. It's all a matter of how far you are willing to travel and how much you are willing to pay. I've already gone over the importance of listening to professionals on audio recordings, but attending a live seminar or conference is taking it to the next level. It's like the difference between listening to a Rolling Stones CD and seeing them in concert. (To my younger readers, the Rolling Stones were… you know what, never mind).

Attending seminars is not only a great way to learn from the experts, but an excellent opportunity to meet people with similar values.

You could also think about joining an organized club or group. You may find a group that is dedicated to something specific that you are looking to grow in: marriage counseling groups, business and investment groups, bible study groups. But it doesn't necessarily have to be. You never know when you can find someone that is a role-model or inspiration for you. You may find someone in a hiking club that can help you to grow in some area of your life. And having that common interest will help you to establish a connection with them to begin establishing a relationship.

If you are dedicated to growth, or making drastic change, then you should have a group that you meet with on a regular basis. A group that will keep you focused, keep you positive, keep you on track. The power of group association is that you can lean on each other and glean from each other. Groups like Alcoholics Anonymous exist to share strength, comfort, and support with its members.

If you can't find a group dedicated to your specific cause or calling, then form one of your own. Napolean Hill calls his inner circle his "Mastermind Group." Success author Glen Bland calls it his "Success Council." There is a limit to how much you can grow in isolation. So start yourself a Mastermind Group; or a club, a guild, a fellowship, a legion…

Social media expands opportunities for association. I feel inadequate talking about social media because I am a tech laggard. Social media websites are a great way to stay in touch with friends, family, colleagues, and ex-girlfriends. Unfortunately, they also give people a sounding board for complaining, griping, harping and any other synonym you can think of for whining.

Most families usually have one crazy relative that will blurt out all manner of profane and offensive things at family gatherings. Thanks to the false sense of anonymity granted by the internet, 90% of people have become that crazy aunt. People, particularly young people, don't think twice about posting something publicly that they would never tell someone to their face; then are surprised when their words come back to bite them.

Don't allow your social media page to become a platform for every moron's hate-filled screed. Block negative comments and if necessary block negative people. And if you want to have some positive association on your Facebook page, try "liking" some positive, successful leaders like John C. Maxwell or Matt S. Law.

My personal experience with association:
I didn't became a Christian until later in life. But even as an opinionated, high school atheist, I had a lot of friends that belonged to Campus Life, a high school ministry organization. I was attracted to them because they were good and non-judgmental people; and because they played volleyball. Even back then, I was seeking to upgrade my level of association.

After college was when I got the opportunity to meet and work with a lot of successful entrepreneurs. Remember earlier when I said "most of us don't have successful, multimillionaire friends with loving family relationships and strong values for us to model ourselves after?" I've actually met quite a few over the years. Obviously, that is the exception rather than the norm, but I can say without question that they have helped me to grow not just in business knowledge but also in just about every area of my life, including leading me to Christ.

It is your responsibility to seek out association with positive people.
It is also your responsibility to cut off negative associations.
The people we spend the most time with, determines which wolf we are feeding.

ENVIRONMENT

Is your everyday environment conducive to feeding the good wolf? As you walk through your home, what do you see? Something which inspires and replenishes the good wolf? Or something that causes you to say, "Oh dear, Lord"? (Not in a spirit of praise and worship but in a spirit of despair).

Any place that you spend a considerable amount of time at, you should strive to make into a positive place, so you are replenished rather than depleted. Your home, you have control of. Your workplace, you may have a little bit of control over. Another place you can control, and many Americans spend a great deal of time there, is in your car.

I spent most of my time writing my first book away from home; usually during my lunch break at work. Because my living space was a disorganized, distracting mess. It was a disaster area.

My bed for example. It was a queen-sized bed, but may as well have been a single because half of it was covered with books and laundry (usually unfolded, clean laundry that I hadn't bothered to put away).

The floor was covered with stacks of stuff. Books, piles of paper, boxes of books and old paperwork. I had no desk to speak of. There was a desk present in the room, there was just no surface area to use on it. There were drawers full of electrical cables that I didn't know what they were for, but I didn't want to throw away in case I needed them. There was trash, actual trash strewn about. Crumpled up receipts, months of mail that I never bothered to open, business cards from people that I had no idea where I met them and would certainly never call them.

Admittedly, I still struggle with disorganization. After publishing my first book, I finally cleaned up my bedroom. It was such a monumental event that I blogged about it. But, over the course of a few weeks, the room began to gradually accumulate more clutter; and my mind followed along.

A cluttered desk is indicative of a cluttered mind. You should keep your living area organized in such a way that it allows you to be focused and productive. Here is a test of how clutter can keep you unfocused. Pretend for a moment that you are at the optometrist, which is clearer, word number one or word number two?

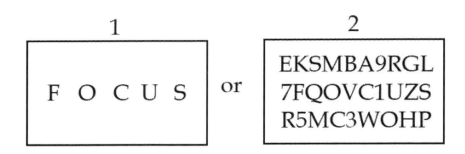

It's the same word. One of them is just more cluttered than the other.

In 2011, a movie entitled Limitless came out. The main character was a struggling writer that came across an experimental drug that exponentially increased his brain's potential. He became incredibly smart. The first thing he did when his brain got supercharged was not immediately start writing his breakthrough novel, or make millions in the stock market. The first thing he did was clean up his pigsty of an apartment. He removed all the clutter. Even a man with a four-digit IQ needs an environment that is conducive to positive thought; an environment that allows him to focus on his project.

De-clutter your environment. The less mess, the less distractions. The less distractions, the greater your ability to focus on what is before you. In other words, I am giving you the same advice that your mom has been telling you for your whole life: "Clean up your room!"

Once you eliminate clutter and distractions, the best thing you can do is give you something to focus on. Ask yourself, "Is this environment helping me to achieve my goals?" Is your mission statement posted in a visible, prominent location? Is it someplace that you see it every day? Do you even have one?

How is your environment detracting from your success? Do you have distractions besides just clutter? Do you have time-wasting activities that arrest your attention? Are you a slave to your X-box, online games, porn?

Let's take a virtual tour of your everyday environment and evaluate it.

Let's start with your bedroom. If you are married then the first thing you see when you wake up is your spouse sleeping and that is the most wonderful and beautiful sight in the world that you will always cherish. Yes it is. If you don't immediately agree with me then work on believing that. It is also the last thing you see before you go to sleep. And the last thing that you see or dwell on or imagine before going to bed is something that will permeate your subconscious mind while you are asleep for the next eight hours (or more like six hours if you are a typical American).

That's why, your bedroom more than any other part of your environment should be a safe, comfortable environment. For those of you that are married, you want to surround yourself with images that emphasize dreams and goals for your family. If you have a family mission statement or vision, have it displayed in a prominent location.

Pay conscious attention to the imagery that you are planting in your mind. Family photos should be happy family photos. Display photos of the two of you from your wedding, or from vacations, where you have nice smiles and you look like you were just clipped out of a magazine ad. Make sure they are photos that you both like. Don't use that Halloween photo where you are pretending to cut each other with a sword and a chainsaw. Yes, it may be funny, but imagery like that is something that you don't want seeping into your subconscious mind every night.

Husbands, don't clutter your bedroom with a bunch of guy-stuff that irritates your wife. Wives, don't make everything pink and frilly.

So far, I've only mentioned visual aspects of your environment. I'm an artist, and I'm a man, so I tend to be more stimulated visually than by anything else. But there are also the other senses to consider when establishing your environment. If you find the sound of oceans and crickets peaceful at night, get yourself one of those cricket-wave machines. Have comfortable sheets and scented candles if that helps you to create a relaxing atmosphere. Remember, those hours spent sleeping with your spouse are forging a deep and devoted bond, so eliminate all irritants and distractions.

Let's move over to your bathroom. Your bathroom mirror is usually the first place you get a good look at yourself in the morning. Because of this, your bathroom mirror is an excellent place to post positive affirmations. In the book *Magic of Believing*, Claude Bristol explains the mirror technique for achieving success. Briefly summarized, you can affect your subconscious image of yourself by looking into your own eyes and stating your affirmations with emotion and conviction. Since you're standing at the mirror, and since you're probably getting ready to start your day or go to bed, why not make your bathroom counter a productive part of your environment?

Attach a note to the wall next to your mirror. If you are feeling particularly daring, write them directly on the mirror with a dry erase marker. You will probably want to change your mirror affirmations, either because they get dirty or accomplished. You also may want to edit it, add to it, clarify it. See the chapter on Speaking for instructions about personal affirmations.

Let's head down to your kitchen and see how you can create a positive environment for feeding your good wolf. Husbands, many wives consider the kitchen "their" territory, so be respectful of making any changes (this is a generalization that is not always the case; also, I am not saying that a woman's place is in the kitchen).

Post photos on your refrigerator. Post photos of your dreams and goals. Everyone goes to the refrigerator several times a day, so that is a perfect spot to hang a reminder of what you are striving towards. Especially if you have a physical fitness goal. Goals need to be placed somewhere that they are seen every day.

Just remember that the kitchen is very often a communal area and guests in your home will most likely see anything on your refrigerator. So make sure that any dreams and goals that you have are those that you feel comfortable sharing and that you are willing to defend (see the chapter on Association).

Let's take a drive in your car. As Americans, we spend an inordinate amount of time driving places. For most of us, our car is a major part of our daily environment. It is also the last thing we see before we get out to start our work day or meet with a client. You should have a positive statement of some sort on the dashboard of your car.

Let's drive over to your office. Your work environment is not always something that you have control over, but do what you can to make it a place that's positive. My opinion on jobs is that they are a necessary evil. I would be hard pressed to find someone that could not think of a single thing they would rather do than be at work at any single moment. But while I may find the concept of a job evil, remember that I did say it was a "necessary" evil (hopefully necessary and temporary).

If you are allowed to make adjustments to your office, cubicle or supply closet, then place reminders of whatever it is you would rather be doing. If you have a work computer, replace the screen saver with those reminders. No, don't ask permission first, just do it. Unless you need help from IT, then pretend you are asking for permission, but really you are asking for assistance. Remind yourself of the things the income from your job makes possible for you to accomplish. Pictures of your family and loved ones. A photograph of a place you want to take them on vacation. A particular quote or phrase that is meaningful to you. A picture that your son drew. Your miniature Bat-signal.

Do what you can to make your work environment empowering to your spirit. Also, having a positive attitude at work will help you to not get fired.

For most people, your phone is also a significant part of your environment. I was a late adopter in getting a smart phone, just like I was late getting a cell phone and late getting internet at home. My tech level usually lags behind the rest of the population by a few years. The next time you're in a public place take note of how many people have their eyes glued to their smart phone. Everyone spends more time on their phones today, especially Generation Y. Their phones take the place of televisions, banks, post offices, and in some cases cars. Because Gen Y is so adept with smart phones and social networks in general, many of them never bother to get their drivers licenses. Certainly a significantly smaller percentage than previous generations.

Since so many people spend so much time staring at that screen, you should place reminders of your dreams, your goals, your visions. The screen background should be something that inspires you. Either a picture or a phrase or a scripture. Your ring tone should be a song that inspires you. If you're from my generation, find a Gen Y kid to show you how to change it.

Make a conscious effort to surround yourself with things that bolster you emotionally. Not just things that are supposed to be inspiring, things that *actually* inspire you. Everyone is motivated by something different.

I am not a Feng Shui expert and you don't have to be one either. Just be aware of your environment; know that it affects you both consciously and unconsciously. Not every single detail of your environment needs to be a spotlight on success and achievement and personal growth. But there should be a combination of things that inspire you and/or have personal meaning for you. Maybe just a painting or piece of artwork that has light and colors that provoke an emotional response from you.

Expend the effort to create an environment that feeds the good wolf.

Highlights from my personal environment:
My current car is a piece of junk. I'm not a car guy. I'll upgrade to a nice car after I fulfill the other items on my list first; or when my mentor tells me, "get a car, you are demotivating your clients." But I do drive, and since I drive and spend time in my car, I keep it at least moderately neat and keep some current goals printed on a 3 x 5 blank index card on the dashboard. Here is my current dash card at the time I am writing this:

Be a blessing to someone today

Feed the Good Wolf

(and some specific business goals)

The reminder to be a blessing to someone is important for myself, because I tend to be wrapped up in my own thoughts in life. While I am that focused on self, I forget to look around at the people around me. To be a blessing doesn't mean I need to drop to my knees and lay hands on a stranger and start a church revival while in line at Starbucks. Sometimes it can be as simple as telling someone, "Hey, I really like your watch."

Also, because I'm an introvert, I need to remind myself to get out of my own head on occasion. It's not that I dislike people, or even that I'm uncomfortable around other people; I'm just equally comfortable being alone. I don't think it's a big deal to go to a movie alone or sit at a restaurant by myself but I forget that other people aren't like me necessarily. Some people are alone and waiting for a kind word from a stranger, or they want some companionship.

Printing "Feed the Good Wolf" is a reminder to myself to only think and dwell on things that are good for my wolf. It is also a reminder that I am writing this book.

Specific business goals are there so that I have something to focus on when I am on my way to a business meeting or visiting a client. It's something worth vocalizing before getting out of my car.

I also like to occasionally put up a quote from my own book, which is a great way to make myself walk the walk (fear of hypocrisy is a great motivator for an author of personal development books).

My home office is in my bedroom. If I had more space and/or a spouse I would move it, but it is what it is right now. Sitting at my computer, let me describe what the wall behind it looks like. There are two small dry erase boards, that I use for daily reminders, or important messages, or notes, or anything important that I feel I might want to add to a book later. Currently, one of them is just filled with a list of chores for tomorrow. There are also three 3 x 5 cards either pinned to the wall or stuck to a board with magnets.

Vision. To help 1 million people to improve their lives financially, relationally, or spiritually.

I am confident.
I am a winner.
I am a success.
Every day my faith and belief are growing.

The last one is a list of yearly goals. Of which I am currently on track to hit two of the four.

Above those is a large poster of a wolf baying. This is a short-term reminder that I am writing a book with a certain wolf theme. I found it online and it was free, so I put it up.

There is also a poster of Jessica Alba. Don't judge me.

Your environment not only says something about you, it says something to you; to your subconscious mind. Make sure that any part of your environment that you have control over is designed to feed your good wolf.

REST

Muscles are pushed then given a chance to rest. That causes them to strengthen and grow. Your mind functions in much the same way. Sometimes you need to take a break from focused activity and rest your mind.

There is a story told about two woodcutters. One was young and strong; a mountain of a man. The other was older, slighter, but wiser. The young man challenged the elder to a competition to see who could cut the most wood. The older man agreed.

The young man grabbed his axe and started chopping wood vigorously. He just set his head down and got to work, knowing that there was no way that the old man could keep up with him.

After a while, the young man noticed that the old man would come wandering back from the far side of his wood shed with his axe over his shoulder and take a break. The young man scoffed. He knew that the old man would never be able to maintain his pace. The young man carried on, cutting wood non-stop. Meanwhile the old man, worked for a while, then took a break. Worked for a while, then took a break.

As dusk approached, the young man thought he had better check on the old man and make sure he was alright. He finally stopped working, sized up his enormous inventory of cut wood and was sure that he must have doubled the amount the old man could do. He walked over to the other side of the woodshed and his mouth fell open. The old woodcutter had a pile of cut timber that was significantly more than he had done.

"How is this possible?" he exclaimed. "I'm much stronger than you and you must have spent half your time resting while I never took a single break!"

The wise old woodcutter smiled. "All that time you thought I was resting? I was sharpening my axe, son."

Your mind can be a powerful tool, or perhaps a powerful weapon (just like an axe). To remain effective it needs to stay sharp. Don't allow it to become dull through repeated and constant use. Also, don't allow it to grow rusty through disuse or watching television.

Take time out for reflection. A lot of authors and speakers talk about looking forward towards your goals (I'm one of them). Remember, "success is the progressive realization of a worthwhile dream or goal." If that is true, then you are already a success once you begin your journey and commit to success. Every day becomes one more victory on the path to your goal. But we still need to take the time to reflect on our progress. Experience does not always lead to growth. We need to evaluate and think on the experience in order to learn from it.

One of the advantages of keeping a journal or maintaining a blog, is that it keeps you constantly in a state where you are reviewing and reflecting on your life. It helps you to put experiences into a clear perspective when you look back on them. Often when you remove yourself from the current emotional turmoil of a situation, it is easier to see the good hidden in the adversity.

Consider dedicating a block of time each week for reflection. Maybe right before planning out your schedule for the upcoming week. Here are some guidelines to keep in mind while reflecting:

1. Wait at least 21 days. A common mistake is evaluating our progress too early with new activities. The fact is, if we are just beginning, we are not qualified to judge the results anyway. At least give yourself a chance to fail before quitting. Beginning a reading program of positive mental attitude books will not yield any drastic change in the first chapter. And you will not see any visible results after your first weightlifting session at the gym. However, performing an activity every day for 21 days is enough time to change your mental self-image and acquire a new habit.

2. Don't get stuck in the past. Reflection time is not the same as pining for

your glory days or wallowing in remorse over poor decisions. Past experience is only valuable when we learn from the experience.

> *We should not look back unless it is to derive useful lessons from past errors, and for the purpose of profiting by dearly bought experience.*
> ~George Washington

Remember, the past is a nice place to visit but you don't want to live there.

3. Reinforce the positive. Every positive experience should be celebrated; and more importantly: evaluated. Identify the behaviors, the habits and the attitude that led to victory so that you can repeat it. It's important to realize that you need to not only celebrate positive results but positive behavior. While on a journey of personal growth, you do not always have tangible results to show for your effort. So celebrate the journey.

If you spent 15 minutes every day for the last week reading a positive book, then that is a victory. Clap yourself on the back, congratulate yourself, recognize that this has been a victorious week for you. When you finish reading your first whole positive book, then that is a HUGE victory. That's why I write short books, so that you can enjoy that victory so much sooner. You're welcome for that by the way.

4. Correct the negative. Reflect on failures, challenges, missteps along the way. Identify the behaviors, the habits and the attitude that led to that failure so that you can avoid it in the future.

Adversity does not always cause us to grow. Adversity only gives us the opportunity to grow.

Ask yourself: What lesson did I learn? How can I apply that lesson to my life? Did any good come out of that situation? Can any good be salvaged from it? What do I need to change in my daily activity?

Reflection on past events converts experience into growth.

Refocus on your goals. Evaluate your activity in the context of your overall goals. Busy is not a virtue. Progress is. Sometimes we mistake being busy for making progress. When we reflect on our past activity, we may discover that we are not progressing towards our goal after all. We may need to refocus our activity to make sure it is in alignment with our goals.

Or during our process of growing we may discover that our goals have changed. I've said before, "Success is the progressive realization of a worthwhile dream or goal." If you no longer feel that your goal is worthwhile, perhaps it's time to change it. When we grow as individuals, our priorities change.

Take time out to reward yourself. Know-it-all authors like myself may tell you that personal growth is its own reward. That's fine, but don't be afraid to give yourself tangible rewards for your commitment and effort. The mule will stop pulling the cart after enough time passes without getting that carrot.

Keep in mind when establishing rewards for yourself that you need to decide on the conditions for the reward beforehand. Don't just say to yourself, "I think I deserve a reward today for all the work I've done." That's an emotional decision and emotional decisions are rarely good ones.

The ability to delay our gratification is a sign of maturity and responsibility. Once you establish rules for rewards, do not cheat! Usually, rewards that we plan for ourselves are small things. And since they are small, they are well within our ability to acquire today; without waiting. This will assuredly sabotage our progress. It's like giving the mule all your carrots then asking him to pull the cart.

I've had some personal trainers tell me that a fitness plan should include a "cheat day." One day a week, the client is allowed to treat themselves to food that is outside of their strict diet. This isn't really cheating. This is a planned reward that you get for sticking to your fitness routine for six consecutive days.

Don't make the rewards too large and too far between. A mule will not pull you ten thousand miles for the promise of an acre of carrots at the end of the trip. The reward is something to coax you towards your goal by encouraging positive behavior. If the goal itself is a long-term or lifelong goal, then it is easier to lose sight of it and give up.

Perhaps you set a goal to go on a Mediterranean cruise. Assuming you are not wealthy for a moment, let's call that a long-term goal. Based on the money that you are setting aside each day and the cost of the vacation package, you see that it will take you 2 years and 4 months to save up the money. Be willing to take some time out to reward yourself a few times along the way rather than wait for 2 years and 4 months. After successfully completing 3 months of depositing your target amount into your vacation account, give yourself some sort of reward (just don't spend money out of your vacation account). You don't have to buy something or spend a lot of money. Take a "you" day.

Take time out to replenish yourself. Choose activities that replenish you, rather than those that deplete you. This will be different for each person. Some people attain tranquility by working in their gardens. Me? I don't like dirt. You can jog, you can meditate, you can read, you can nap. At my home in Hawaii, people surf. To them, that is a replenishing activity. Myself, I've never been a strong swimmer so going to the beach is not particularly relaxing or replenishing for me. After swimming I am wiped out and dehydrated. And sometimes burnt. And salty. And my pockets are full of sand. I am deplenished after going to the beach (that's not a real word, I checked).

Find out what energizes you. Back in college, if I was depressed or angry (which I was a lot of in college), I would stop at the Humane Society and spend about half an hour playing with cats and kittens. I called it "fuzz therapy," and I recommended it to many people over the years (I apologize to all the psychotherapists who lost their client base to a bunch of kitties).

Some of your hobbies may shift from replenishing to depleting, but you may continue to do them out of habit or expectation. Perhaps you have a weekly bridge game, but over the years the group has turned into a bunch of bitterly-complaining old men and at the end of the night you find yourself edgy and irritable. You may want to think about switching what you do with your bridge night. Sometimes, when we begin a leisure activity we enjoy it immensely at first; then when we start to develop some skill, enough to start taking it seriously, we start berating ourselves for screwing up or performing poorly. (cough *golf* cough). Quit.

I often equate exercising the mind with exercising the body. Include some time to rest your mind in your personal growth plans. Feed the good wolf a steady diet rather than allow it to gorge.

PRINCIPLES

When your character is pure, it requires less effort to police your behavior.
~Matt S. Law

Business and sales techniques may change from time to time. Success principles are constant and unchanging. Sound financial principles such as spending less than you earn and using your saved pennies to invest and allow the earnings to compound over time so that your money works for you. These principles have been around since before the birth of Christ. The idea that your life will always move in the direction of your dominant thought? Thousands of books have been written about that subject. You get what you speak? All over the Bible.

I was warned through much of my life, "Never follow a man. A man will always disappoint you, because they are human. Always follow the principles of the man."

So when seeking input, when feeding your good wolf, never follow someone blindly, never seek out tricks or gimmicks or snazzy quotes and sound bites. Always concentrate on principles.

Honesty. There is no growth curve or skill development in being an honest person. There is only the decision. It is entirely within your power to be honest in your day to day dealings. At all times, choose the truth.

> *Whoever is careless with the truth in small matters cannot be trusted with important matters.*
> ~Albert Einstein

While one lie does not make you a dishonest person, all too often one lie begets another lie, which begets another lie. If you tell one lie, there is always the possibility you will need to repeat it to someone else. Or the need to create another lie to bolster the first. And of the recipient of the first lie telling it to someone else, not knowing that they are perpetuating a lie. The longer a lie is allowed to live, the more shame and humiliation it brings not just to you, but also to those who were unwilling participants in the lie.

> *Three things cannot long be hidden: the sun, the moon, and the truth.*
> ~Buddha

A lie is short-sighted. All lies are selfish. Can you think of an example where a lie is not used to protect yourself from harm or to gain something you don't deserve?

Honesty is universally admired. From the folk tale of young George Washington chopping down his father's cherry tree to the fable of the boy who cried wolf. Just as dishonesty is universally condemned in all cultures and beliefs.

> *No legacy is so rich as honesty.*
> ~Shakespeare

Make a holy resolve to be an honest man or woman. Not to be "more" honest. Simply be honest. The next time temptation comes to you to tell a lie consider the harm it does to your character.

The next time you tell the truth even though it causes you embarrassment, harm, or suffering, it pays you considerably more in terms of character. By accepting the consequences of the truth, you become something greater.

Speak aloud: Liars are greedy cowards. I choose to be an honest person. I will speak the truth. Each time I face a situation that can potentially harm me, I will speak the truth and feed the good wolf.

The greater the potential harm you may receive from speaking the truth, the greater the return in character. The good wolf increases in power. What you may lose in reputation, you will gain in character. Through continually choosing truth over convenience, soon the strength of your character will overwhelm the shadow of your reputation, until honesty becomes a trait associated with your name.

Almost any difficulty will move in the face of honesty. When I am honest I
never feel stupid. And when I am honest I am automatically humble.
~Hugh Prather

Seek truth. Share truth. Spread truth. Deciding on honesty feeds the good wolf.

Perseverance. Perseverance is steady persistence in the course of action, especially in spite of difficulties, obstacles, or discouragement.

If you have a worthwhile goal, fix it firmly in your mind, then go. Once you begin, press on. Once you take your first few steps you gain momentum, you gain confidence. When you hit your first obstacle, and you will hit one, go around it. Persevere.

Many of the great achievements of the world were accomplished by tired and
discouraged men who kept on working.
~Unknown

The story is told of a legendary American-Indian rain dancer. People all across the lands repeated the story that he had a perfect record; every single time he performed a rain dance ceremony, there was always rain. Several chiefs gathered together their shamans and holy men for a gathering where they could all learn the secret of this rain dancer. At the gathering they all talked about their techniques, their processes, their preferences. When it finally came time for the rain dancer to speak and reveal his secret, he just shrugged and said "I just keep dancing until it starts raining."

It's not that I'm so smart, it's just that I stay with problems longer.
~Albert Einstein

When you climb your first mountain, whether actual or metaphorically, you have conquered that mountain. Say it out loud, "I have conquered my mountain." Conquering one gives you the confidence and the experience to conquer the next.

You will struggle through adversity. You will overcome weakness. Every step closer makes you stronger. Every difficult step, even stronger. When faced with an obstacle that looks impossible to cross, you assess, determine, deny its insurmountability and persevere. The greater the risk or difficulty of your voyage, the more tremendous the victory. The more glorious your character shines.

> *Not only so, but we also glory in our sufferings, because we know that suffering produces perseverance; perseverance, character; and character, hope.*
> ~Romans 5:3-4

Every time you strive forward and persevere with the anticipation that you will make it, you feed the good wolf.

Responsibility. No one should ever talk about their rights without recognizing their responsibilities. That is the sign of an immature and selfish person. The man that invokes his rights while neglecting or not considering his responsibilities deserves no respect and rarely receives any.

> *With great power comes great responsibility.*
> ~Ben Parker

Consider a company that takes no responsibility for its products or service. They will—and should—go bankrupt. How about a politician that makes claims and promises then takes no responsibility for failing to live up to or fulfill a single one? They should get the pink slip when up for re-election (although that doesn't always seem to be the case).

When we take responsibility for something—a plan, a promise, an action—we accept ownership. We tie our names and our words to its successful completion. We accept the consequences and we don't try to shift the blame.

Only the most arrogant and selfish of people would take responsibility for their successes while pawning off the responsibility for their failures on others.

You are responsible for your actions. You are not a slave or a mindless automaton. You can think and act of your own accord, therefore you are accountable for your actions. By what you eat and drink, you take responsibility for your own health. By your daily activities, you take responsibility for your physical fitness. By your reading, you take responsibility for where you focus your intellect on a daily basis. You are no slave, you are your own master. With freedom comes responsibility. You are responsible for your own life.

When you fail to fulfill your promise, you apologize to the injured party, accept responsibility and do what you can to make it right. Your character shines more brightly because of it. You will take responsibility for your mistakes. If you cause harm you will acknowledge fault and try to rectify your mistake. Even the one you hurt will admire your acceptance. Passing the blame on to someone else does not lessen the hurt to the injured. It is just a futile attempt to protect your own feelings or reputation.

> *Our deepest fear is not that we are inadequate. Our deepest fear is that we are powerful beyond measure. It is our light, not our darkness, that most frightens us.*
> ~Marianne Williamson

You accept your responsibility gladly. You choose to be a responsible person. And in so doing, you feed the good wolf.

Kindness. It costs nothing to be kind, but a simple act of kindness can impact someone for the rest of their life. A compassionate smile from a loved one, a word of admiration from a stranger, a nod of acknowledgment from a superior can bolster the fearful and weary.

You never know when someone is on the verge of quitting, on the edge of despair, or are moments away from suicide. Sometimes a single kind word or a heartfelt compliment will pull them back from the darkness. Acts of random kindness are all it takes to make our world as close to heaven as it can get.

When you love someone, you treat them kindly. But also recognize that by being kind to someone, you expand your capacity to love. The two go together, but one doesn't always precede the other.

Have you ever performed a good deed, a favor, a random act of kindness to some stranger for no particular reason? Didn't you feel good about that later? That's because at the core of human nature is the desire to do good; to be men and women of character; to serve others rather than to be served.

As the law of sowing and reaping takes over, all your kindness will be returned to you multiplied many times over. Routinely performing kind acts, turns into a habit of kindness, which in turn develops into a kind soul.

Anytime you can give another person's spirits a lift, or imbue him with more life and energy, you are performing a small miracle.

> *Perhaps you will forget tomorrow the kind words you say today, but the recipient may cherish them over a lifetime.*
> ~Dale Carnegie

Generously dispense words of kindness. People treasure them more than physical wealth. By being kind to others not only do we feed our own good wolf, we also provide food for the good wolf within those others.

Discipline. Discipline is the ability to delay the gratification of desire for future benefit. Living a disciplined life means living in the moment but keeping focus on the future.

> *Right discipline consists, not in external compulsion, but in the habits of mind which lead spontaneously to desirable rather than undesirable activities.*
> ~Bertrand Russell

Discipline is not about denying the self for the sake of denying pleasure. It is about denying those activities that cause long-term harm to the self. It is about having a body and mind that operate properly. It is about improving rather than diminishing the self. Discipline is willingness to deny the lesser for the sake of the greater. It is seeking happiness rather than just pleasure.

A disciplined man is not a glutton. He recognizes that moderation in his diet will prevent a stomach ache minutes from now and possibly an extra inch of fat for the rest of his life. Be disciplined enough to recognize that you cannot eat anything you want whenever you want. Eat healthy foods in healthy portions. There is a saying about the people in Hawaii, "we don't eat until we're full, we eat until we're tired." That is not discipline. Man eats. Beasts feed.

A disciplined man is not a spendthrift. He recognizes that his long-term financial health can be damaged by irresponsible spending. He recognizes that emotional purchasing decisions are rarely good ones. He knows that pennies saved are not only pennies earned, but that those saved pennies will actually work for him and multiply through sound investments. The disciplined man will save first before he spends; and never ever pay interest on depreciating assets. Earn interest, do not pay interest.

A disciplined man is not wasteful with his time. Don't tick away the moments that make up a dull day. Don't fritter and waste the hours in an offhand way; kicking around on a piece of ground in your hometown, waiting for something or someone to show you the way. (Okay, I admit that was a paraphrase of the first verse of *Time* by Pink Floyd, but the message is still valid).

Invest your money, but also invest your time. Money investments return more money. Time investments return timeless values if you invest into your own character or that of your children. The disciplined man will do the important things first, the selfish things when he has free time.

A disciplined man does not indulge his bestial nature. A disciplined man is capable of controlling his sex drive. He isn't compelled to pursue every woman he sees like a dog. Sex is a beautiful act of love between you and your spouse. Man loves. Animals breed.

A disciplined man is slow to anger. A moment of rage can damage a relationship permanently. It's the small man that raises his fists in anger. Resorting to violence is the last resort of the disciplined man, but an early option for the weak-willed. Yelling at a child or loved one can wound as deeply as a physical assault. Words spoken in anger can cause irreparable damage to someone's self image. There is a reason that profanity is called a curse. Be disciplined enough to control your tongue.

The long-term harm of a lack of discipline is exponentially greater than the immediate cost of discipline. The disciplined man feeds the good wolf and starves the bad wolf.

No life ever grows great until it is focused, dedicated, disciplined.
~Harry Emerson Fosdick

Humility. Humility insulates us from pride. C.S. Lewis calls pride the greatest of sins because it leads to all others. The greater the person, the greater their vulnerability and the greater their fall from pride. The sin of pride caused Lucifer to rebel against God and be cast out of heaven.

True humility—the basis of the Christian system—is the low but deep and firm foundation

of all virtues.
~Edmund Burke

To be humble is to be honest with yourself. To be humble is to admit your own shortcomings, your mistakes, your weaknesses. Only by being honest can you recognize your own faults and only by admitting them can you address and correct the problem. That's why humility is considered the foundational virtue.

Humility is the foundation of all the other virtues hence, in the soul in which this virtue does not exist there cannot be any other virtue except in mere appearance.
~Saint Augustine

Without humility we run the risk of an inflated ego. Ever notice how someone with a long history of being a loser that gains some small amount of success becomes insufferable? Have you seen someone that is awarded great success at a young age without having to strive or sacrifice to attain it? It is why child stars and heirs to great fortunes have a tendency to self destruct. The ones that don't are those that are firmly grounded with a sense of humility.

Humility does not mean thinking less of yourself either. I am no better than anyone else. I have certain gifts and talents but they only make me more or less suited to certain situations. I do not view myself in a negative light. After all, I am important. I am a child of God. I am inherently valuable and priceless. I have a soul. But so does that homeless person. When you have a perspective of humility, you see the value in all people. It's why humility leads to compassion and compassion to charisma.

By placing value on others we position ourselves to greatly impact them in a positive way. Only once did Jesus say that he was setting an example for his disciples. It was when he was washing their feet. If I were walking on water, curing disease, casting out demons, and raising the dead; I could see myself having trouble remaining humble.

Without humility, any other values you instill in your children will eventually be lost to pride. With a false sense of one's own greatness, they will feel entitled to the kindness of others without the obligation to be kind to them in return. Same with discipline, same with perseverance. How many people put into a position of power and prominence feel that they no longer need to be honest or take responsibility for their actions?

To be humble to superiors is duty, to equals courtesy, to inferiors nobleness.
~Ben Franklin

Humility is not just food for the good wolf. It's also antitoxin that prevents the poison of pride from killing or corrupting it.

STARVE THE BAD WOLF

To develop strength of character we need to feed the good wolf. But to eliminate flaws in our character, we also need to starve the bad wolf. "Starve the Bad Wolf" is an equally important half of the wolf-feeding parable; but would have made the title too long for a 6 x 9 inch book cover.

Everyone has heard the comparison that the human brain is like a computer. A computer is only as valuable as the input it receives. While we are loading quality programs into our computers, we also need to keep the negative from corrupting our hard drive. We should be just as careful of what we put into our brains as we are of what goes into our computers. If you never install virus protection on your computer and you visit a bunch of sites with dubious reputations, then you deserve to have your computer be sluggish, not secure, and prone to viruses. And if you don't protect your brain from negative influences, then you generate negative thoughts; and your brain becomes sluggish, insecure, and prone to sickness.

Here are some areas of life that I would recommend most people should either restrict or eliminate completely from their lives in order to stop feeding the bad wolf.

Television. The first time I counseled someone to cut their television cable to save $50 a month he looked at me like I had just suggested cutting off his arm and selling it. It may sound like I am some sort of highly disciplined taskmaster when it comes to my own life's schedule and priorities, but even I watch television on occasion. According to the A.C. Nielsen Co. though, the average American watches over 4 hours of TV a day. That's 28 hours a week or 2 months of every year. Could you imagine if that same American used that time for something constructive like building a business, developing a skill or hobby, or talking to his children?

My main problem with television is not that it consumes over one-sixth of the average American's life; it's that during that four hours a day it is almost exclusively feeding the bad wolf. Almost all television programming is negative today. Compare the values of the average TV family today to the values of the 1950's and 60's TV family. Compare the language. Do you want your child to be more like Richie Cunningham or the kids from South Park? Do you want your family to be more like the Cleavers or the Bundys? If a child spends more time with a television than with a parent, then that child's primary provider of moral guidance is the television.

Consider some issue where your values differ from your parents. Most of the time, your new and improved value is not something you came up with reading philosophy or through deep thought and meditation; it came straight from Hollywood. If your values are determined by pop culture then they are not values at all, they are popular opinion; and opinions change all the time. If you grew up in Nazi Germany and watched nothing but Nazi television you would probably think that that system of values was perfectly fine.

If you think that TV-watching time is family time, then I would challenge you to replace it with real activities and interactions with your spouse and family. If you think that you need to watch TV to be able to have conversations with your friends, then I would argue that you need to start having either real conversations or real friends.

Television producers are not your friends. Their only interest in you, is to keep you partially-hypnotized in front of the screen so that large corporations can sell you stuff.

Newspapers. The newspaper industry has been steadily dying so I should probably refrain from kicking it on its way out the door. In today's internet age, anything that makes it into print is already old news. In today's environmentally-conscious age, young people don't like the idea of chopping down a forest just to print news that's already been tweeted to the point of monotony. And in today's information age, it has become increasingly obvious that newspapers rarely print objective facts but agenda-driven opinions.

Despite all these issues, my main problem with newspapers is that they predominantly print bad news, because bad news sells. "Well, that's the way of the world," you may think, "It's just full of grief and tragedy and destruction." But I contend that the reason bad news sells is because so many things in the world are good and right. For example, living in Honolulu, I would not bother to pick up a newspaper if the headline reads "Sunshine Tomorrow." But I will stop in mid-stride and read it if it says "Snowstorm Tomorrow." Sunshine is the norm, so Snowstorm sells. Good in the world is the norm, so evil sells. If the news is 90% negative, it's because the world is really 99% positive.

However, inputting a steady stream of negative news into your mind only serves to feed the bad wolf. Always hearing bad news creates an expectation of bad news. It makes you cynical and pessimistic about life.

We can endure almost any misery as long as there is an end to it in sight. When is the last time the news gave you an account of all the world's troubles and then ended with a solution for them? The worst thing you can do to your subconscious mind is fill it with bad news then go to sleep so that you can dwell on it for 8 uninterrupted hours.

The news media is not your friend. Clip your coupons, read the comics, do the crossword then throw out the rest.

Negative Association. I covered this negative in the chapter on Association. Just remember that you will become like your peers. If your parents are not still selecting your friends and keeping the bad kids away from you, then that responsibility is yours.

You may have some negative people that you call friends. If they spend all their time dumping garbage on you, then you need to reevaluate whether they consider you a friend or just someone to accept their bullying.

Video Games. The video game industry brings in more revenue than movies, television and radio combined; and has been doing so for the last ten years or so. Unfortunately, like movies, television and radio, many games feel the need to push the envelope of the rating system as far as it can go.

If man is a product of both genetics and environment, then how can anyone possibly think that it's a good idea to spend any length of time in a video game environment surrounded by graphic death and destruction? I would be willing to bet that in a few years there will be an epidemic of video-game-induced PTSD; although it will have a brand new name so that a psychologist can publish a paper and take credit for diagnosing this "new" mental disorder.

But there is another aspect of video games outside of graphic content that is feeding the bad wolf. The allure of video games is that they create the "illusion of achievement." In most games you play a character that develops skills, acquires wealth, unlocks secrets, gains power, defeats the enemy. As human beings we are designed to be goal-striving organisms; we are happiest when we have a sense of purpose. Except that all that skill, wealth, and power exists only as electronic data bits that can all be wiped out by forces outside your control. You are spending hours and dollars developing a game persona that is both fictional and temporary.

Some men die by shrapnel, and some go down in flames,
but most men perish inch by inch, playing at little games.
~Unknown

Video game companies are not your friend. They are farming you for dollars and giving you just enough of a feeling of self-satisfaction to keep you logged in.

Pornography. Just as video games became a substitute for real world achievement, pornography is the substitute for real world intimacy and relationships.

I'll just talk to men on this subject since they are the main customers of the porn industry. Most men think of pornography as no big deal, as a victimless crime, as a harmless (albeit embarrassing) behavior. After all, it's not as damaging as being hooked on drugs or alcohol or cigarettes. But porn can be addictive. The reason it is so addictive is because it connects with something primal within the male spirit, and that is the pursuit of a woman.

There is truth in the aphorism that behind every successful man is a successful woman. Napoleon Hill, in *Think and Grow Rich* devotes an entire chapter to the "emotion of sex," and how it is squandered by young men. He cites how love for a woman is what has driven many extremely successful world-changing men through history from Lincoln to Napoleon. John Eldridge, in *Wild At Heart*, identifies "a beauty to rescue" as one of the three longings of the male heart. Pornography saps the will of men by robbing them of one third of their heart's purpose.

Attraction to and desire for a woman is normal, but when it becomes perverted it becomes potentially harmful. Pornography has been linked in many studies to increased violence against women. Even if viewing porn doesn't turn a male into a sexual predator, it will certainly increase his appetite for physical sex; and in most relationships, the male already has a greater sex drive than the female. Increasing that gulf can never add harmony into a marriage, can it?

To put this into the shallow male perspective, let's say that your wife develops an unhealthy affection for gardening. Every day she watches television programs of couples pulling weeds together. Even though you used to help garden on occasion, she becomes obsessed with having you pull weeds with her. She asks you into the garden first thing in the morning, again right when you get home from work, then again after dinner. She keeps badgering you that it is healthy for couples to work together in the garden. She begins comparing your performance to the male gardeners on the websites she visits and you don't measure up; you just don't seem as eager and willing as you once were. How long do you think it will be before she finds someone else to tend her garden?

Anything that you implant in your mind remains there permanently. You may think that pornography is a harmless escape into fantasy, but subconsciously you will always be comparing your wife to the professional women that are so much more willing and eager to please their partners. Watching porn cheapens your mental image of your wife and your marriage.

Porn peddlers are not your friend. They make money off of your desperation and loneliness and sometimes addiction. And at the risk of sounding obvious, that woman performing sex for dollars is not your friend either.

FINAL THOUGHTS

A great man once said, "The solution to pollution is dilution." Imagine that your mind is a reservoir of pure water, and that all the negative that the world offers is a black, disgusting fluid. Left to its own devices, the natural world will occasionally dump a load of negative into your pool. Once that negative is poured in, it can't be separated from the water. Since you can't remove the pollution from the reservoir that is your brain, your only option is to try to dilute its influence by pouring as much fresh, pure water into it as you can.

When you realize that your character, the sum total of the features and qualities that define you as an individual, is the result of the thoughts that you allow yourself to dwell on, you should become ferociously protective of what you allow into your mind.

Keep pouring clean water into the reservoir through what you read and what you speak every day. Continue to filter your water by controlling who you listen to and who you associate with. And stop letting the world dump that smelly black stuff into your pool.

> *And now, dear brothers and sisters, one final thing. Fix your thoughts on what is true, and honorable, and right, and pure, and lovely, and admirable. Think about things that are excellent and worthy of praise.*
> ~Philippians 4:8 (New Living Translation)

The purpose of feeding the good wolf is to build ourselves from the inside out. To establish a firm foundation of character within our lives, not through tricks or gimmicks, but by changing our daily thoughts. Not to conceal our faults but to eliminate them by starving the bad wolf. Not to exaggerate our strengths but to truly grow them through steadily feeding the good wolf with positive thoughts.

As you grow yourself, by continuing to feed the good wolf, you will become a greater person. Then you also will begin to attract other great people. There is a universal law as certain as the law of gravitation that says: You will not attract in your life that which you want, but that which you are. By developing yourself into a person of strong character, you will attract other people of strong character.

As you continue to feed the good wolf in your heart, you will also become an example for others to follow. Through your actions, through your integrity, through the continuing building of your character, you will help to feed the good wolf in others; and eventually, others will begin to see the value in feeding their own good wolf.

Soon you will not be a lone good wolf. You will have your own wolf pack.

Through synergy, you will increase your ability to positively impact other people. Encourage and share with others. Be a source of positive. Pass along your teachings.

> *Everyone thinks of changing the world, but no one thinks of changing himself.*
> ~Leo Tolstoy

To change the world, first change your character
To change your character, first change your thoughts
To change your thoughts, feed the good wolf in your heart.

Be Blessed in All Things.

ABOUT THE AUTHOR

Matt S. Law has been a student of life and success for nearly twenty years and is recognized as an expert on the subjects of motivation and personal growth. He received his BA in Art from the University of Hawaii, which has nothing to do with the direction of his life currently. In addition to being an entrepreneur, he has worked as an illustrator, a graphic artist, a barista, a salesman, an actor, and a writer. He discovered that his calling is to be not just a teacher, but a teacher of subjects that are actually applicable and vital for success in life. Math is not in that category.

Read more from Matt S. Law at his blog
http://mattslaw.wordpress.com/

Made in the USA
Middletown, DE
12 April 2017